The Men's Guide to Power Napping

John Moynihan

Also by John Moynihan

To
Bill Carrington

Napper extraordinaire.

*"My stuff isn't Tolstoy quality, but I do take pride in
the work I do."*

Tim Ferriss
Feb. 4, 2014

Table of Contents

Start

Introduction

This book is a celebration of the power nap.

The power nap, as I define it, is a short, concise nap of about 20-30 minutes of actual sleeping time.

Really, no more than that.

This is about the amount of sleep time that various health experts tell us we need every day to refresh and recharge our batteries. Any more than that and the sleeping becomes a long slog, really a sleeping event unto itself. We're not talking about sleeping all afternoon here.

The power nap is not that.

It is short and quick and to the point. It comes on fast. It gives us immediate energy. It is totally beneficial and life sustaining.

Most young guys don't need to nap. They have the energy to go strong all day, like Russian bulls. For these lucky lads, I would say that they can briefly page this little book for a few nuggets that may prove helpful for that hangover they encounter after a weekend in Las Vegas.

For the rest of the men out there in the world, the nap is more necessity than luxury and reading this book is essential.

This is written for all of us male toilers out there in thankless, grinding jobs, men with young kids, wives, and dogs that need walking at all hours of the day and night. Men that are burdened with the many responsibilities of ordinary and routine life.

For us, the nap is an elixir.

A recharge of life.

Like plugging your iPhone 6 into a pristine wall outlet for an hour's charge to top off the battery. Nothing feels better!

Enough philosophizing. Let's get into the meat of the matter.

The Zen of Napping

True Zen philosophy has the whole riddle thing going on.

It has to be hard before it gets easy.

Classic things like that leave you scratching your head and saying:

"What the heck does that mean?"

There are a lot of little parables or tales in the Zen world that are called koans.

These are little stories that focus in on the essence, the core, of true Zen philosophy.

The most timeless one is finding the sound of one hand clapping.

So, the small boy goes to the Zen master and asks him to tell him the way to enlightenment.

The monk tells the boy to go out and find the sound of one hand clapping and bring it back and describe it to the monk for verification.

The young boy is puzzled. He searches for six months and finds nothing. He hears the sound of children playing. He comes back and describes that to the monk. The monk says "No, that is not the sound."

Again the young boy goes out into his surroundings and searches for the sound of one hand clapping.

He comes back to the monk and describes the sound of birds happily chirping in the forest. He thinks he has found the sound. The monk again says "No, that is not the sound of one hand clapping."

The boy does this three more times, coming back to describe the sounds of the wind, the trees rustling, and the sound of the waves crashing on the beach. Each time he is rebuffed by the Zen master.

Distraught, the boy finally comes back and says that he has exhausted it all. He has searched high and low in the world for the sound of one hand clapping. And he was not able to find it. The sound was everywhere and nowhere. It was ephemeral.

It was at that point that the monk finally told the young boy that he was starting to hear the sound of one hand clapping.

The young boy finally understood.

The Zen of the perfect power nap is essentially the same path as searching for the sound of one hand clapping.

You will know it when you achieve it.

Tools of the Trade

Tools

It's somewhat random to think about "tools" in the context of taking a nap.

You think WTF—just shut my eyes and sleep. I don't need any tools. But you'd be wrong and also missing the point.

There are only a few tools absolutely essential for a good nap.

The good news is that several of them you already have at your disposal.

The others are easily accessible.

And cheap. Very cheap.

You don't have to go to Home Depot or Lowe's to buy the tools that I am describing for a perfect nap. These tools are simpler to access and purchase.

So what are they, these magical and mystical tools of the napping trade?

They are the following: the right mental attitude, no ego, a warm and comfortable sweater, a good pillow, and a fleece blanket.

That's it. These are the workman's tools for the perfect power nap.

Now it's true that you don't need to have every single item for a great nap. But having a set of good working "tools" around your house or base of operations, just increases your odds of having a great nap every time. Like a skilled carpenter with his box of essentials.

And if you're going to commit to napping, then you want your naps to be short and successful.

Since the power nap is 20-30 minutes, you don't have much time to make mistakes or more to the point, not fall asleep.

If you have your tools at the ready, your chances of success increase dramatically. Plus, if you're taking up power napping, you want to become a pro. A true professional. An Olympic napper. A guy that can throw down a nap at a minute's notice.

These tools will help you achieve your goal of a short, quick nap.

Let's deconstruct each tool individually on the following few pages.

Mindset

The mindset of napping.

This is the single, most important tool by far that you need for a great nap.

Simply, a good head.

This is taking your mind to a spiritual place, a place of relaxation and comfort.

One of the biggest problems for Americans is that we are all Type A compulsives. Doing things, getting things done, working hard, keeping our families together, all the hard stuff of life. Once you are in that mode, it is hard to stop.

To successfully nap, you've got to relax and let it flow.

Think of the image: taking your fist and opening it up and spreading your fingers wide.

It's the concept of total relaxation.

It's basically like meditation. Only easier.

With meditation, you concentrate and bring your mind to a different level of consciousness. There is some focus and concentration needed to get there.

With napping, it's just letting go--and falling asleep.

You can't fight it by thinking about getting a cup of coffee or standing up and walking around.

You have to do the opposite. You have to encourage it.

Let the sleep urge wash over your body and take hold of you.

And then, you fall asleep.

No Ego

What the hell does no ego mean?

Don't worry, I'm not going to throw a lot of pop-psychology drivel at you.

This is a practical guide to taking the perfect nap.

So you need the answer quickly and clearly.

No ego means you can't be afraid to look foolish while you're napping.

So what does looking foolish mean?

Sometimes a little drool on your pillow. Yeah, that's right. Accepting that little wet spot of saliva if you just pass out and go into immediate sleep. It happens sometimes.

It also means looking incredibly bad and unattractive.

There is also the problem of the open mouth.

When I nap, I often open my mouth. A lot of people do it. Without question, it is the most unattractive view of me (or anybody else!) possible in the world.

It looks like I am dead. Or passed out drunk. Or shot with a tranquilizer gun, like a bear in a tree.

It's a very common problem. I often start with my mouth closed when I nap, but it droops open along the way, after I fall asleep. The facial muscles relax and I'm off to the races.

It is bad stuff!

If your wife sees you sleeping with your mouth open, she'll likely never find you attractive again. But this is a guidebook on napping, not on looking good or maintaining your marriage.

Mouth open sleeping is never attractive. It's a corrosive look. Even attractive women who nap or fall asleep, often drop their jaw and sleep with their mouth open. They don't look good either.

So having no ego simply means being comfortable with people seeing you asleep, at your most vulnerable, with your mouth agape.

More about mouth open sleeping in a bit.

Warm Sweater

A comfy sweater is critical.

It's that simple.

I call it my Frank Sinatra sweater.

It's the kind of sweater you saw him in when he was in his prime in Las Vegas in the 50s and 60s.

Not in the photos of him in glamorous casinos and nightclubs on the Strip on Las Vegas Boulevard where you would see him with the full Rat Pack. In those scenes he'd have on a really cool suit, a skinny tie and a fedora.

But there's a whole round of other photos, where you'd see him cavorting with starlets and girlfriends behind pools or off in the California or Nevada desert, when it was cool at night or in the early morning.

In those scenes, he'd wear a light sweater just to take the chill off.

Not bulky, but just enough.

I'd also call it a golf sweater or a light Polo sweater.

That's what you need to mentally get in the mood for a great nap. To create that warm, soft cocoon for the upper half of your body, your core. The word is schoochy.

Core comfort is critical for good napping. And a good sweater sets the foundation here.

There are, of course, many variations on a theme for sweaters. If you're napping in Portland, Maine in the winter, then you'll need a thick, heavy sweater that really takes the cold out. Good quality LL Bean fits the bill here. This is true even if the house or car you're sleeping in is seventy degrees. It's a state of mind.

If you're napping in Florida on a seventy degree day, then the light Polo sweater with Merino wool is likely for you. That's my favorite sweater, hands down.

Don't get carried away, if it's hot out, you obviously don't need a sweater. But oftentimes you do want one. Trust me. The sweater just makes it better and that much easier to fall asleep.

Perfect Pillow

I have a bad neck, a really bad one.

In all honesty, who doesn't??

Not surprisingly, many guys do. Particularly older guys.

It comes from working the machine, my body, that golden temple, hard for many years.

Playing sports in my youth, lifting babies, raising kids, walking dogs, carrying groceries up two flights of stairs for thirty years, painting on ladders, repairing houses, lifting junk into mini-vans.

They all contribute.

Not to mention the most common actual ailments we have with our lumbar and cervical spines, including degenerative disease, spinal stenosis and herniated discs.

It's the progression of life.

These problems are all very real and sometimes very painful.

In the world of napping, you've got to treat your neck with care to avoid problems with your neck. Either actual problems that you have now, or avoiding problems in the future.

The best way to account for a bad neck is to nap with the perfect pillow.

A perfect pillow is just that—a pillow that gives you amazing stability and comfort. It supports your cervical spine and carries the weight of your head perfectly.

Unfortunately you've got fluffy, firm, flat, foam, fat and feather pillows from which to find your perfect pillow.

I don't need to write any more about the perfect pillow. In the Zen tradition, you'll know it when you find it.

Like falling in love.

Or getting a good dog.

For me, the perfect pillow is a rectangular, flat one, no more than two inches thick. I like my neck to be almost flat when lying down.

So I keep that small, thin pillow handy in my favorite napping spot and whip it out when the urge to nap washes over me.

Do I need a perfect pillow to nap? Probably not.

But having it around and using it most times, makes napping that much easier and perfect!

Fleece Blanket

The fleece blankie.

Are there two more perfect words in the English language? Probably not.

Fleece Blankie.

Perhaps "summer lease" is a close second for the world's most beautiful phrase.

But for a napper, the fleece blankie is the sine qua non.

The ultimate napping tool.

There is something about a fleece blanket, in dark blue or green, that makes a napper want to nap. A full size one fits comfortably over your body while you are lying down on the couch or sitting in a chair. It is a perfect fit.

A fleece blanket envelopes you in softness and comfort, like you are back in the womb.

It's warm and inviting.

The term "schoochy" comes to mind when describing the feel of a good fleece blanket.

If your house is warm, why use a fleece blanket? You're thinking that you don't need it. That it's superfluous.

But the fleece blankie has little to do with warmth. And it's far from superfluous.

You use it to help get into a sleep state more quickly, and stay there restfully.

Wrap it over you, crawl under it, let it envelope you. Succumb to its powers.

The fleece blankie is there to provide comfort and warmth.

Use it to create the best sleeping environment and experience for a perfect power nap.

Other Tools

There aren't any.

There are no other tools absolutely essential to a perfect nap.

None.

Not a single tool.

There really aren't.

Just get your comfy sweater, your perfect pillow, your fleece blankie, find a quiet spot somewhere and go nap.

So those are the basic tools you need for a really great nap. Use them or not, the choice is yours. You don't need them to fall asleep. But if you have them in your toolkit, you'll be able to take a nap more quickly and the nap will absolutely be more restful and regenerative. Trust me on this.

That is it.

Power Napping:

The Keys to Success

Don't Fight It

Keep it simple, stupid.

KISS.

This is the number one key to success for power napping.

If you want to nap, nap.

Don't fight it. If you have the urge to fall asleep, then just do it. Fall asleep.

Heed the call of those heavy eyes.

Now sometimes, it's not socially appropriate or possible to nap when you want to. For example, you can't nap while you're driving your car. And you often can't nap while you're at work. But you can pull your car off the road into a parking lot or rest area and grab a fifteen minute nap. I do it all the time.

Whenever the opportunity presents itself to nap, you should. Don't put up feeble resistance. Just fall the hell to sleep.

I sometimes come home from work, bone tired, after crunching numbers all day as a financial services middle manager. I am exhausted. I am so tired that I fall right over on the couch and sleep for twenty minutes. No shit. Right down with a knockout punch when I come home. That little nap I take is rejuvenating. I charge my battery for the rest of the night and I am good to go.

I also nap in the afternoons on weekends. Exhausted from the work week (is there a theme here??), I will take a short nap in the afternoon. I can usually take this nap in the car at BJs while my wife is shopping, or on the couch or in a movie theatre. Head down and napping for 15-20 minutes, it's a pure recharge.

So, Rule Number One—if your body is telling you it's ready to sleep, don't fight it. Just fall asleep.

This, of course, isn't practical in every situation, particularly in the working world. Most jobs, whether old school or new school, don't have provisions for you to take a nap. A few do, but it's rare.

So you may have to improvise. That means napping in your cube, in your car, in the stairwell, on a pile of packages, or on the bus or the train to and from work. Cover up your wallet and iPhone so they don't get stolen, however, if you're napping while riding on public transportation. It can easily happen. And try not to miss your stop.

But the general principle of when tired, take a nap holds true pretty much always if you want to be a successful napper.

The Art of Sleep

You may have to train yourself to fall asleep easily.

And this isn't always so easy.

I don't need a dark room to nap in. To the contrary, I like falling asleep in the sun, like a dog in the summer. I put my face right up toward the sun, or under a light if I am in a chair or on a couch. The light radiates through my closed eyelids and I see bright reds and oranges. I like sleeping in the light. But I still have to focus in the light to fall asleep.

You have to do the same thing.

Focus on falling asleep. This means thinking happy thoughts that induce you to fall asleep. Like thinking about lying on a chaise at a deserted beach on a cove in the Caribbean. Or sailing gently in the sun, a gentle breeze on your face. Or whatever your happy place is. You get it. You've got to take your mind to some relaxing, fun place. Transport yourself.

The good news is that falling asleep is a lot easier than meditating, for example.

When you meditate, you have to first assume the meditation position. Then start repeating your mantra, quietly to yourself, over and over. But if your mind drifts over to some useless and annoying monkey thought, you've got to bring it back to center and continue having no thoughts. That's like learning to hear the sound of one hand clapping all over again.

Falling asleep is a hell of a lot easier.

Just get into a comfortable position, close your eyes and think pleasant thoughts.

The next thing you know, you've been sleeping for 15-20 minutes.

Perfect. You are totally recharged.

Does life get any better?

Short Naps

Naps need to be short and to the point.

This is a very important aspect of napping.

If you keep your naps short, they're not a hassle.

So they don't take up a large part of your time. You can work around them.

You can get a great nap in twenty minutes and still be able to accomplish a lot in your day.

If you're able to integrate a little power nap into your day seamlessly, then you will have achieved the Zen of napping.

You can be a productive member of society and still get a nap in every day. You can maintain your job. You can stay married. You can still be a father. Once you learn to power nap effectively and are able to weave it into your daily routine, you are golden.

You will feel great, be healthy and remain productive.

Productive and healthy—the American dream.

Regular Naps

Regularity—as in every day—is another key to napping.

You want to train your body to nap every day, if possible.

Develop your body rhythm.

It's a beautiful reinforcing technique that becomes a virtuous cycle. Your body wants that short, extra sleep in the middle of the day to recharge, so it shuts down at that point to force you into the sleep mode.

You sleep for 20-25 minutes and bingo—you're refreshed.

It's not hard. It's essentially like recharging your iPhone in the middle of the day for thirty minutes. Your body will train itself to need that little sleep break after lunch and crave the short nap.

That's perfect. You need to reinforce that response, where your body is looking for a short nap in the middle of the afternoon.

You reinforce a good habit.

I know that during the working week it is usually impossible to take a nap in the middle of the afternoon unless you work at some place like Google where they have nap pods or other silly stuff like that. But even at Google, who's really going to nap in the middle of the day when you're making $200,000 a year?? You can't put that kind of money in jeopardy.

So, sneak out and nap in your car.

My point is that it may not be practical to nap every day in the working world in the afternoon.

But it's a solid goal to have, something to shoot for. Certainly you can do it on your days off, on holidays, and on weekends.

Seize The Opportunity!

Seize the moment when it comes to napping.

You absolutely need to nap when the opportunity presents itself. It may not be the ideal nap spot or nap time, but you've got to take it when you get it.

Just yesterday I was with my family on the tourist trolley from downtown Tampa to Ybor City. I had finished lunch and the Florida sun was hot. The streetcar was old and it was incredibly uncomfortable with tiny wooden seats. I put my head back and fell asleep right in the seat. My head was tilted back resting against the glass window. Brutally uncomfortable, almost painful. But I was able to fall asleep for 10-15 minutes. It wasn't my perfect nap, but it was the best I could muster under the circumstances.

You get my point.

Say you're in a doctor's office waiting to get your bum knee checked out for the 100th time. The urge to sleep comes upon you. Your eyelids get heavy and you start to drift away. Don't fight it. Tuck your arms in, drop your head, relax and fall asleep. They'll wake you up when it's your turn to see the doctor. And she'll likely be late anyway.

Nap on the train in the morning as you go to work if you're still tired, nap at lunch, nap on the way home in the carpool or on the bus.

The opportunity to nap often comes in strange places and at curious times.

Doesn't matter.

Seize the opportunity when it arises and take that nap!!

I've napped in back seats. I've napped in church. I've napped in rest areas off the highway. I'll nap anywhere I can when the situation presents itself.

And you should too. Seize the moment. Nap when you can!

Classic Nap Venues

The Couch Nap

Cocooning, fetal position, pulling a fleece blankie up to your neck…

The couch nap is the gold standard of napping.

You can't get any more comfortable than napping on a couch.

Hopefully it's a couch in your living room, where it's warm and quiet. Your wife and the kids have gone out to see the latest Disney movie for the afternoon and for a little while, it is just you and the couch.

It doesn't happen often, but when it does, you have to seize the moment. Enjoy it whenever you can.

The couch nap is the Vatican, the Wailing Wall and the Mecca of napping, all rolled up into one venue.

I have a few tips for a couch nap to insure your success.

First, have your tools at the ready so that when the opportunity presents itself for an afternoon couch nap, you are as fast as a bolt of summer lightning. I keep my favorite blankie and pillow right in the living room closet, on top of all the other junk in the closet, so that I can pull them out quickly, without having to move a lot of hats, gloves, and jackets. You can't lose the moment by having to search out your tools under the vacuum cleaner.

Second, clear the couch of all the little decorative pillows that your sister-in-law gave you with embroidery. The ones that talk about family love. Kick them to the floor and get a clean work space. Act like a surgeon.

Three, tuck your legs up and assume the fetal position. Immediately.

Drop your head onto your most comfortable, hand-selected pillow that you positioned perfectly for sleep.

Pull your fleece blankie up to your neck, or over your head if you prefer, open your mouth and have at it.

Sleep for twenty minutes and wake up totally refreshed.

It's that simple.

The Car Nap

The car is a beautiful spot for a power nap.

You're waiting to pick up your kids from a party or a school event that you didn't attend and you're fifteen minutes early.

Or your wife is shopping in TJ Maxx's for couch pillows.

Or you are waiting for your daughter at the train station and she texts you that the train is running thirty minutes late.

Perfect.

All of a sudden there's a twenty minute window that opens up to you. The opportunity presents itself. Perfect for a car nap.

When I'm having a car nap, the first thing I do is lock the doors. I automatically hit the door lock button with my left index finger and bingo, I'm safe and sound in my little cocoon. You don't want to be robbed or have something stolen from the back seat while you're sleeping.

Or even worse, get shot.

I guess a crazy person can still shoot you through the window, but at least it feels safer. Plus, with the doors locked and the tinted glass that's in most cars nowadays, nobody can see you and you're safe inside.

Next, go horizontal. I immediately reach over and drop the seat all the way down to a comfortable position and lay flat in the seat. Total comfort. Plus, nobody can see you at that point. You're invisible.

A major benefit here is that you don't have to support your head as it rolls around leaning against the window glass or the void between the door and the seat or the totally uncomfortable headrest if you're trying to nap while you are sitting up.

The critical element in a car nap for me is support of my head and neck. My big squash. It is incredibly easy for me to get a crink in my neck if I don't stabilize my head and neck first. It's too much loose weight rolling and lolling around.

I frequently use my jacket or sweater or arm or whatever I have lying around in the car to support my head and stabilize it for my nap when I'm horizontal.

Then unlock your seat belt because you're not going anywhere and get comfortable!

No one can see you, the car looks empty and you're safe and sound in your locked vehicle, comfortably napping.

Does it get any better? Likely not.

Close your eyes, and enjoy twenty minutes of pure perfection.

The Plane Nap

The hardest nap in the world is the plane nap. No doubt about it.

People, noise, tight seats and plane movement all conspire to make this the most difficult nap.

But it is a big venue for napping for a lot of people, particularly business folk.

There are generally two types of people in the world: those that can sleep on planes, and those that can't.

It's not easy to successfully nap on a plane as aviation engineers design airplane seats to be absolutely uncomfortable. Total torture devices. It must be a required design criteria.

At least I find them that way.

Nevertheless, I am able to nap for 10-20 minutes at a time on a plane, if I work at it.

But it's not easy.

Obviously, window seats help.

You can slouch against the window and sidewall of the plane and sleep that way. But it's frequently cold if your face is leaning against the window and air is typically blowing down on you from the upper sidewall vents.

A blankie, jacket, hoodie, or pillow is almost a required item for a nap in a plane.

Once again, you have the critical element of supporting your head. The ten to fifteen pounds of dead weight of your squash has to be dealt with. You need to lock in place to comfortably fall sleep.

At least that's true for me. Once I can get my head supported, I can nap on a plane.

Which brings up those awful looking foam donuts, what I call plane pillows, that people use as neck braces for plane sleeping and napping. I've tried them and I don't find them comfortable or really supportive for my neck. Plus, they're a pain in the ass to carry with you onto and off the plane.

And it goes without saying that you look incredibly dorky walking around in an airport with a foam neck pillow, let alone how bad you look actually wearing one.

Now on flights, you have to pay for a blanket, so few people do that. It's also hard to find the little foam giveaway pillows on planes today and if there are any, others scoop them up immediately. Or again, you have to pay for them and who pays for a pillow on a plane?

So your best solution here is to get on the plane wearing a fleece jacket that you can bunch up and use as either a head and neck support or a back support.

This is your essential plane napping tool.

And if you're not napping on the plane, you can always wear the fleece jacket to stay warm.

Airplane seat hierarchy for napping is obvious.

Window seats are best, although they are pretty uncomfortable spots as well, truth be told. If you need to get up, you need to mobilize two other people first.

Middle seats are second best or worst, depending on your outlook. The main problem with a middle seat is that you're not able to slouch left or right in the seat because you end up invading the air space of the person next to you.

And aisle seats are probably the toughest spots in which to nap.

Aisle seats expose you to constant jarring throughout the flight.

I'm over six feet tall and the second I try to nap in an aisle seat and slouch to the left, my shoulder starts getting hit by the flight attendants or just rude passengers. It's inevitable. It's the same with your knees, legs, and feet.

You're guaranteed to get whacked unless you bring yourself into a tight, self-compressed ball in your seat.

Some people drop their tray table and nap sitting down with their head in their arms on the tray. I've tried this technique, but find it too uncomfortable.

For successful plane napping, I lean back in my seat with my fleece jacket supporting my head and neck, stretch my legs straight out under the seat, and cross my arms and hug my torso. Open my mouth slightly, and with a bunch of deep, slow quiet breaths, fall asleep for twenty minutes. Bingo.

Key plane tips: keep your head supported throughout your nap and stay within your allotted space in your seat to avoid getting jostled by other people or worse, bumpy air.

Get these two items right and you will more likely be able to have a successful plane nap.

Good luck.

The Office Nap

The office nap is a beautiful thing.

But, like a unicorn, does it exist in real life?

The office nap is supposedly okay in hip, new wave places like Google and Zenefits and Microsoft.

They sometimes have places to nap that they call nap pods. Or nap stations.

Be careful here. If the boss catches you napping when you should be reinventing your global sales and social media strategy, you are in trouble.

Where's Bill for this meeting? Oh, he's napping in a nap pod.

Once people know that about you, you are toast.

The nap pod is definitely not on the road to the CEO's seat.

If you are sitting in a cube, it's tough to nap in place because all your co-workers are right next to you, doing work.

So another possibility is to go out to your car if you drive to work, and nap in it for fifteen minutes. Just use the car nap tips described earlier to insure your success.

Car napping in your office business park is more acceptable, but it's still partly dangerous if some of your peers see you sleeping in your vehicle. Word gets out fast and spreads like an unwanted STD.

A good defensive strategy here is to make sure you drop your seat all the way down, so you're sleeping horizontal, and nobody can see you taking a nap. This cuts down on your exposure significantly.

Of course, you can always drive your car off campus and sleep in the Safeway parking lot. This is a lot safer, but it takes time to get there, fall asleep, wake up, and drive back. So it becomes the hour nap and that is not efficient. Nobody has that luxury in these modern times. Nobody.

Now if you are old school with an actual old school office with a door, just close the door and nap. This is probably okay and people will soon figure out you're napping and leave you alone.

I knew a guy who was paranoid but still napped in his office. He would close the door, lay down on the floor, and put his feet against the closed door. That way, nobody could knock and just barge in and catch him napping.

Kudos to him for creating that defensive posture and napping strategy. You can't deny a man his nap.

So, office naps are sometimes possible, but not usually.

And they can be dangerous to your career.

Caveat emptor here.

The Chair Nap

The chair nap is the last of the classic nap venues.

It's easily the most common place to take a nap because for most Americans, we're sitting down almost all day, whether at work or at home.

The chair nap breaks down generally into two different styles—comfortable chairs and non-comfortable chairs.

The non-comfortable chair nap is usually a nap taken at the kitchen table, in an office or occasionally, in a church pew.

The defining characteristic of all these places is that the chair you are napping in is generally very uncomfortable and non-supportive.

The keys for success here are several. First, support your head and neck so your head isn't rolling around everywhere. Do this by tucking your neck in and placing your head in the classic down position. Secondly, tuck your body parts into a self-supporting posture. Cross your arms over your chest and tuck your hands into your armpits. Next cross your legs with one leg over the other for support.

Then close your eyes and nap. Usually you fall asleep instantly because your body is craving a nap—otherwise you wouldn't be falling asleep in an uncomfortable chair. The key is to create enough support to sustain you for the twenty minutes you need for an energy recharge.

The other type of chair nap is one that is taken in a comfortable chair, say in your living room or in a hotel lounge.

The same basic principles apply as above—create an environment of body support so that you don't wake yourself up in five minutes because your head falls off to the side.

I generally stretch out when taking a nap in a comfortable chair and extend my body as much as possible. My head goes back and is supported by the top of the chair. My legs go out fully and straight and I cross my feet. If there is a small pillow around, I put it behind my lower back for support. My arms are straight down and I cross my fingers and rest my hands on my lower lap.

This is the classic, comfortable chair napping pose, the money shot for napping.

Your main body parts are supported in a comfortable chair nap, so just close your eyes and enjoy.

Random Nap Tips

Squash Weight

The average human head weighs in at around ten plus pounds and I'm sure mine weighs twenty pounds as a thick-headed Irishman.

It is absolutely critical that you support the weight of that giant gourd on top of your body while you nap.

Your squash.

The weight of one's squash is often overlooked but it's like a bowling ball that is situated on top up there.

And it's constantly rolling around while you are napping.

Nothing is worse than having a crinked neck when you wake up from a nap. A crinked neck comes from having your head or neck in an awkward position and sleeping with it that way for 10 to 20 minutes.

That's why I talk about the perfect pillow. To keep your squash supported and in a good place while you nap.

Supporting your head and neck is probably the simplest but most critical element of successful napping.

Be sure to do it right.

The Sun

I love to nap in the sun.

Just like any old housecat on the planet.

Or a dog as well.

We are all base level creatures that enjoy the sun.

The sun is sugar for me. I love being out in the sun, enjoying its warmth and light. We all do.

So naturally, I like napping in the sun and I'm really multi-tasking when I'm doing it.

I'm getting a nap in to recharge my batteries but I'm also getting exposure to the sun and vitamin D and all the beneficial aspects that go with it.

I'm a pale Caucasian guy. My roots are from Northern Europe and my heritage is Irish and Polish. They don't make a guy with whiter, paler skin.

So when I nap in the sun, I also get sun burned easily.

My cardinal rule is to always use sunblock when napping in the sun. You should too. The sunblock I use is SPF 70 -100.

I also put a hat over my face if I am napping directly in the sun, say on a beach.

For me, there is nothing worse than a sun burned face from twenty minutes of pure summertime sun exposure from a nap.

Enjoy the gain and avoid the pain. Use sun block or cover up when napping in the sun.

Mouth Open or Closed?

Here's the story line simply summarized.

Pro:

When you open your mouth you can fall asleep quicker, and oftentimes easier.

The air seems to be able to flow more easily into your lungs through the open passageway.

You sleep more fully and soundly.

Con:

You look like a stupid dork sleeping with your mouth open.

That's it. Now you decide. You can successfully nap either way and it's strictly up to you and personal preference.

Tough decisions abound in life.

Top Tips Redux

Cocooning. The nest. Hat. Support the head and neck. Short. Heavy eyes. Don't fight it. Fetal position. Tools. Sandwich action.

If you want to nap successfully, you've got to overcome your ego and just dive into taking a nap.

Put away your worries, restraints and fear of looking foolish while you sleep and just do it.

That's what this book is all about—how to nap successfully.

So, in that vein, here are my top tips restated:

Prepare Mentally—Always get in the right frame of mind. Check your ego at the door. Mentally, be in a calm relaxed mood to nap. Go to your happy place in your mind for sleeping. Dissipate whatever anger or irritation you may have from your psyche and open your mind to the possibility of a quick revitalizing sleep experience, a short nap.

Assume the Position—Don't be embarrassed to get into your most comfortable napping position. This is all about you and recharging your cosmic battery. So it may be sleeping on the couch in a tight fetal crouch. So be it. It may be lying in the car in the TJ Maxx parking lot in the sun, completely horizontal. Go for it. Or it may be sitting in your chair in the living room, head sideways, mouth slack and you snoring. If so, just drop your jaw and let the air in.

No Timer Needed—Once you get proficient at napping, you can actually train your body to sleep for just twenty minutes or so. Don't ask me how or why or the medical implications behind it, but your body is like a good dog—treat it right and it will respond. If you do enough twenty minute naps, it will regulate itself into that body rhythm so you wake up in twenty minutes and not sleep for two hours.

Use Your Tools—Pull that fleece blankie up over your head, get into that wonderfully comfortable warm sweater, build a cocoon with pillows, put a pillow over your head, or put a pillow behind your lower back. Use whatever tool you have in your tool box to have a totally successful nap.

Enjoy the heat, it can't be beat—Sleeping in the sun is wonderful. But be careful. Throw the baseball hat over your face or load up on sunblock or do both, so you don't get sunburned.

Engineer the Nap—Napping sometimes is not easy to fit into your busy day. Or it's frowned upon by your peer group. It doesn't matter. You still need to engineer a short 15-20 minute nap into your existence as often as you can, hopefully daily. Nothing is more vital to your good health.

Close the door and let it roar—A lot of times when you're napping, you're snoring. This is another little beautiful body function. Don't worry about it. If you're snoring, you're snoring. It's not romantic, but your wife and family are probably used to it anyway.

Support Needed—Be sure to support your head and neck when you nap. Nothing is more painful than a whacked neck from napping in a bad position. Support your lower back and arms and legs as well if you need to. Provide whatever support you need to fall asleep comfortably.

Don't be a fool, check for drool—Lastly, sometimes when you dive deep for a nap, you're drooling. Bad stuff. When you're in sleep mode your body just takes over and you are a slave to it. Check your little sleeping pillow after a nap for drool and clean up after the fact if you need to.

Bottom Line—Do whatever it takes to have your best nap. You know what gets you to fall asleep and nap the quickest and what conditions give you the best, strongest and sweetest naps. Just replicate those conditions time and time again. Don't stop. Keep doing it.

That's it. Enough proselytizing.

Go take a nap.

Conclusion

Nap

So this was my short love story to the nap. That most glorious of PG rated activities.

The ultimate restorative.

These were my musings on how to nap and where to nap and the tips, traps and techniques that I always use to have a good nap.

Hopefully, some of these ideas resonate with you as well and you pick up one or two tips to help make your naps better, easier to do and more satisfying.

Remember, the goal here is to nap on a short and regular basis.

Twenty minutes is the ideal amount of time for a power nap in my opinion and experience.

It's just enough time to re-energize your body and give you that boost that will take you through the day and into the night. Any less, and it's not helpful. Any more, you're groggy.

Napping is not a substitute for a night of solid sleep, by any means.

It's designed as a quick fix. An energy supplement that doesn't bring toxins into your body.

And did I mention that it's free and easy?

You don't have to spend $5 for an energy shot of sugary goop or a cup of overpriced, boutique coffee.

A nap is free, and nothing but pure goodness.

So I'll end this little book on the same note on which it began.

You don't need a book to nap.

So put this little tome down, close your eyes and fall asleep for twenty minutes in the comfort of your favorite chair.

And enjoy every moment.

About the Author

John Moynihan is a Boston based author, investor and financial services professional. He has worked at world class organizations including AEW Capital Management, Fidelity Investments, and Sun Life Investment Management.

He is the author of a variety of books including Thirty Minute Fitness, The Boomer Survival Guide, Wampum Nation and The One Hour MBA. He lives in Brookline Village, Ma.

Visit the author at johnjmoynihan.com
And FreshPondBooks.com

Printed in Great Britain
by Amazon